the best of Jewel

Cover Photo © Suki Dhanda / Retna Ltd.

ISBN-13: 978-1-4234-1685-2
ISBN-10: 1-4234-1685-6

HAL•LEONARD®
CORPORATION

7777 W. BLUEMOUND RD. P.O. BOX 13819 MILWAUKEE, WI 53213

In Australia Contact:
Hal Leonard Australia Pty. Ltd.
4 Lentara Court
Cheltenham, Victoria, 3192 Australia
Email: ausadmin@halleonard.com

Visit Hal Leonard Online at
www.halleonard.com

AGAIN AND AGAIN

Lyrics by JEWEL KILCHER
Music by JEWEL KILCHER and JOHN SHANKS

Lis - ten, dear, ___ I need you to hear; ___ I can - not
Walk down the street, stare at lots of ___ things ___ that pass in

dis - ap - pear, ___ I've tried a - gain and a - gain and a - gain and a - gain.
stead - y streams ___ a - gain and a - gain and a - gain and a - gain.

I know we said that we'd give up, ___ said we'd had e - nough ___ a -
Do what I should, try to stay bus - y; ___ your face is all I see, ___ a -

BREAK ME

Lyrics and Music by
JEWEL KILCHER

I will meet __ you in some place __

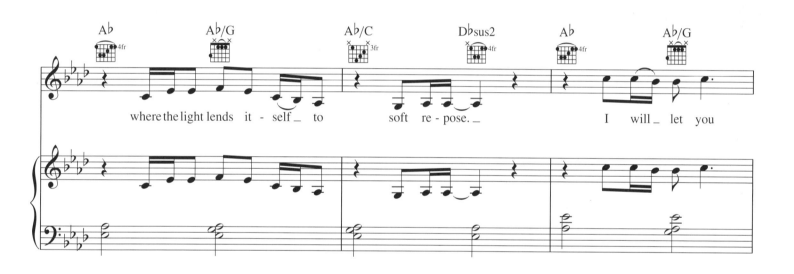

where the light lends it - self __ to soft re - pose. __ I will __ let you

un - dress me, __ but I warn you I have thorns like an - y rose.

DOWN SO LONG

Lyrics and Music by
JEWEL KILCHER

* Originally sung an octave lower.

FOOLISH GAMES

Lyrics and Music by
JEWEL KILCHER

Slow

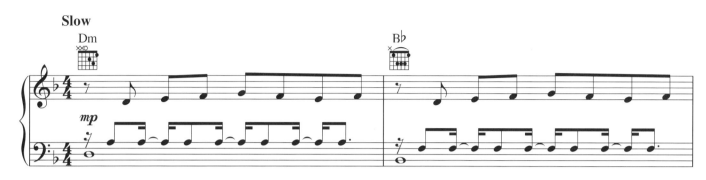

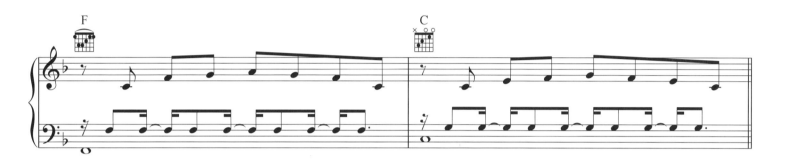

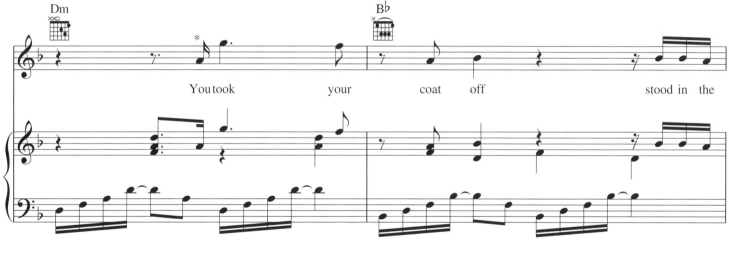

You took   your   coat off   stood in the

rain; _____   you're al - ways cra - zy like _ that. _

* *Originally sung an octave lower.*

GOODBYE ALICE IN WONDERLAND

Lyrics and Music by
JEWEL KILCHER

D.S. al Coda

but you o - pened up __ my eyes. __   So

CODA

life.   Grow-ing up is not an ab - sence of dream - ing; it's

be-ing a-ble to un-der-stand __ the dif-f'rence be-tween the ones you can hold __ and the ones that you've __ been sold. __

_____   And dream-ing is a good thing 'cause it brings new things to life, but pre-

they are on-ly a ___ re-flec - tion ___ of my lone-ly mind ___

___ find - ing, ___ they are on-ly a ___ re-flec - tion ___ of my

lone - ly mind ___ find - ing. ___

I found ___ what's miss-ing in ___ my life.

poco rit.

INTUITION

Lyrics by JEWEL KILCHER
Music by JEWEL KILCHER and LESTER A. MENDEZ

HANDS

Lyrics by JEWEL KILCHER
Music by JEWEL KILCHER and PATRICK LEONARD

If I could tell the world __ just one thing __ it would be __ that we're all o - kay. __ And not to wor - ry, 'cause wor - ry is waste - ful and use - less in times __ like these. __

* Originally sung an octave lower.

JUPITER

Lyrics and Music by
JEWEL KILCHER

* Originally sung an octave lower.

STAND

Lyrics by JEWEL KILCHER
Music by JEWEL KILCHER and LESTER A. MENDEZ

STANDING STILL

Lyrics by JEWEL KILCHER
Music by JEWEL KILCHER and RICK NOWELS

2 BECOME 1

Lyrics by JEWEL KILCHER
Music by JEWEL KILCHER and GUY CHAMBERS

I watch_ you while_ ___ you're sleep - ing, mess - y hair, chest bare, ___ moon-light on your

WHO WILL SAVE YOUR SOUL

Lyrics and Music by
JEWEL KILCHER

People livin' their lives for you __ on T __ V. __ They say they're better than you, __ and you a-gree. __ He says "hold __ my calls" from behind those cold __ brick walls says, "Come here, boy, there ain't noth-in' for free." __

Originally sung an octave lower.

YOU WERE MEANT FOR ME

Lyrics by JEWEL KILCHER
Music by JEWEL KILCHER and STEVE POLTZ